D1357898

Presented to:

Emaline Lapinski

From:

*Christian Education
Committee*

May 5, 2009

Presented to

On the Occasion of

From

Date

THE LITTLE BOOK OF
LOVE

Compiled by
CYNTHIA MARGARET STOKER FRANKLIN

BARBOUR
PUBLISHING, INC.
Uhrichsville, Ohio

Dedicated to my husband,
Darryl, who has been the
blessing of true love.

© 2001 by Barbour Publishing, Inc.

ISBN 1-58660-116-4

All Scripture quotations are taken from the King James Version of the Bible.

Published by Barbour Publishing, Inc., P.O. Box 719, Uhrichsville, Ohio 44683
http://www.barbourbooks.com

Printed in Canada.

Contents

Every single act of love
bears the imprint of God.

Familiar acts are
beautiful through love.

PERCY BYSSHE SHELLY

I love these little ones,
and it is not a slight thing when they,
who are so fresh from God,
love us.

CHARLES DICKENS

The most important thing
a father can do for his children
is to love their mother.

The God Who made your children
will hear your petitions.
After all, He loves them more than you do.

JAMES DOBSON
Parenting Isn't for Cowards

Every man is rich who has
a child to love and guide.

Our Daily Bread

Give a little love to a child,
and you get a great deal back.

JOHN RUSKIN

We can't form our children
on our own concepts;
we must take them and love them
as God gives them to us.

JOHANN WOLFGANG VON GOETHE

God gave us free choice because
there is no significance in love
that knows no alternative.

Bread of Life

Choose your love,
love your choice.

THOMAS S. MONSON

Love conquers all things.

<small>VIRGIL</small>

Nay, in all these things
we are more than conquerors
through him that loved us.

ROMANS 8:37

God is love, and to die means that I,
a particle of love,
shall return to the general and eternal source.

LEO TOLSTOY

I would rather live and love
where death is king than have
eternal life where love is not.

ROBERT G. INGERSOLL

But I say unto you, Love your enemies,
bless them that curse you,
do good to them that hate you,
and pray for them which despitefully use you,
and persecute you.

MATTHEW 5:44

But love ye your enemies, and do good,
and lend, hoping for nothing again;
and your reward shall be great,
and ye shall be the children of the Highest:
for he is kind unto the unthankful and to the evil.

LUKE 6:35

Love is the circle
that doth restless move
in the same sweet eternity of Love.

ROBERT HERRICK

But as it is written,
Eye hath not seen,
nor ear heard,
neither have entered into the heart of man,
the things which God hath prepared
for them that love him.

1 CORINTHIANS 2:9

Fate, time, occasion, chance, and change?
To these all things are subject but eternal love.

PERCY BYSSHE SHELLY

To be able to say
how much you love
is to love but little.

PATRARCH

Tell someone you love them,
tell them again,
tell them again.

A new commandment I give unto you,
That ye love one another;
as I have loved you,
that ye also love one another.

JOHN 13:34

"Love thy neighbor"
is a precept which could transform the world
if it were universally practiced.

MARY MCLEOD BETHUNE

By this shall all men know
that ye are my disciples,
if ye have love one for another.

JOHN 13:35

Brotherly love is
still the distinguishing badge
of every true Christian.

MATTHEW HENRY

Bring love into your home,
for this is where our love
for each other must start.

MOTHER TERESA

This is my commandment,
That ye love one another,
as I have loved you.

JOHN 15:12

There is no exception to
God's commandment
to love everybody.

HENRY BUCKLEW
Daily Spiritual Vitamins

Be kindly affectioned one to another
with brotherly love;
in honour preferring one another.

ROMANS 12:10

Love must be as much a light
as it is a flame.

HENRY DAVID THOREAU

Love kindled by virtue
always kindles another provided that
its flame appear outwardly.

DANTE

Love is an act of endless forgiveness,
a tender look which becomes a habit.

PETER USTINOV

People need loving the most when
they deserve it the least.

JOHN HARRIGAN

And love can come to everyone;
the best things in life are free.

LEW BROWN & BUDDY DE SYLVA

Freely we serve,
because we freely love,
as in our will to love or not;
in this we stand or fall.

JOHN MILTON

As long as we are loved by others,
I would say we are indispensable;
no man is useless while he has a friend.

ROBERT LOUIS STEVENSON

Nothing we do, however virtuous,
can be accomplished alone;
therefore, we are saved by love.

REINHOLD NIEBUHR

Always leave loved ones
with loving words.

Write down the advice of him
who loves you though you like it not
at the present.

SPANISH PROVERB

No love, no friendship,
can cross the path of our destiny
without leaving some mark on it forever.

FRANCOIS MAURIAC

A best friend is someone who
loves you when you forget
to love yourself.

He who sows courtesy
reaps friendship, and
he who plants kindness
gathers love.

St. Basil

Greater love hath no man than this,
that a man lay down his life for his friends.

JOHN 15:13

The love we give away
is the only love we keep.

ELBERT HUBBARD

Love gives itself;
it is not bought.

HENRY WADSWORTH LONGFELLOW

True love's the gift
which God hath given
to man alone beneath the heaven.

WALTER DILL SCOTT

Love is the greatest thing that God can give us,
for He Himself is love;
and it is the greatest thing we can give to God,
for it will also give ourselves.

JEREMY TAYLOR

All love is sweet,
given or returned.

PERCY BYSSHE SHELLEY

One may give without loving,
but one cannot love without giving.

Always give people
a little more love and kindness
than they deserve.

God gives us love;
something to love He lends us.

ALFRED, LORD TENNYSON

Love has nothing to do with
what you are expecting to get;
it's what you are expecting to give—
which is everything.

Therefore thou shalt love the LORD thy God,
and keep his charge,
and his statutes, and his judgments,
and his commandments, alway.

DEUTERONOMY 11:1

The measure of God's love is
that he loves without measure.

St. Bernard

God must love the common man;
He made so many of them.

ABRAHAM LINCOLN

The God of love
my Shepherd is.

GEORGE HERBERT

All loves should be
simply stepping stones to
the love of God.

PLATO

Nor height, nor depth,
nor any other creature,
shall be able to separate us from the love of God,
which is in Christ Jesus our Lord.

ROMANS 8:39

Riches take wings,
comforts vanish, hope withers away,
but love stays with us. God is love.

LEW WALLACE

For the Father himself loveth you,
because ye have loved me,
and have believed that I came out from God.

JOHN 16:27

Jesus said unto him,
Thou shalt love the Lord thy God
with all thy heart,
and with all thy soul,
and with all thy mind.

MATTHEW 22:37

Love is an image of God,
and not a lifeless image,
but the living essence of the divine nature
which beams full of all goodness.

MARTIN LUTHER

Love is an image of God,
and not a lifeless image,
but the living essence of the divine nature
which beams full of all goodness.

MARTIN LUTHER

God loves us the way we are,
but too much to leave
us that way.

And we know that all things work together
for good to them that love God,
to them who are the called
according to his purpose.

ROMANS 8:28

Jesus answered and said unto him,
If a man love me, he will keep my words:
and my Father will love him,
and we will come unto him,
and make our abode with him.

JOHN 14:23

The supreme happiness of life is
the conviction that we are loved,
loved for ourselves,
or rather loved in spite of ourselves.

VICTOR HUGO

They say a person needs just three things
to be truly happy in this world:
someone to love,
something to do, and
something to hope for.

TOM BODETT

To love is to
place our happiness in
the happiness of another.

BARON GOTTFRIED WILHELM VON LEIBNIZ

Love one another, and you will be happy.
It's as simple and as difficult as that.

MICHAEL LEUNIG

Love seeks to make happy
rather than to be happy.

RALPH CONNOR

Happiness is the spiritual experience
of living every minute with
love, grace, and gratitude.

DENIS WAITLEY

Joy is love aware of
its own inner happiness.

FULTON J. SHEEN

Love is the master key
which opens the gates of happiness.

OLIVER WENDELL HOLMES

The heart that
has truly loved never forgets.

THOMAS MOORE

And hope maketh not ashamed;
because the love of God is shed abroad
in our hearts by the Holy Ghost
which is given unto us.

ROMANS 5:5

One loving heart
sets another on fire.

St. Augustine

The heart that loves
is always young.

GREEK PROVERB

The heart of him who truly loves
is a paradise on earth;
he has God in himself,
for God is love.

ABBE HUGO FELICITE DE LAMENNAIS

Real love is
helping someone who can't
return the favor.

Love is all we have,
the only way that each can help the other.

EURIPIDES

Jesus, on the other hand,
loves you regardless of whether
you are naughty or nice.

But God commendeth his love toward us,
in that, while we were yet sinners,
Christ died for us.

ROMANS 5:8

Life with Christ is endless love;
without Him it is a loveless end.

BILLY GRAHAM

Nails could not have kept Jesus
on the cross if love
had not held Him there.

Our Savior, Who is the Lord above all lords,
would have His servants known by
their badge, which is love.

HUGH LATIMER

We love the Lord, of course,
but we often wonder what He finds in us.

EDGAR WATSON HOWE

If we love Christ much,
surely we shall trust Him much.

THOMAS BROOKS

The best portion of a good man's life
is his little, nameless, unremembered
acts of kindness and love.

WILLIAM WORDSWORTH

Life is short.
Be swift to love,
make haste to be kind.

HENRI F. AMIEL

An ounce of love is
worth a pound of knowledge.

JOHN WESLEY

And to know the love of Christ,
which passeth knowledge,
that ye might be filled with
all the fulness of God.

EPHESIANS 3:19

We are not made for law,
but for love.

GEORGE MACDONALD

Love is the lesson
which the Lord us taught.

EDMUND SPENCER

Love is the hardest lesson in Christianity,
but for that reason,
it should be the most our care to learn it.

WILLIAM PENN

What most people need to learn in life
is how to love people and use things
instead of using people and loving things.

Love has always been
the most important business of my life.

HENRI BEYLE

You will find,
as you look back upon your life,
that the moments when you have really lived
are the moments you have done things
in the spirit of love.

HENRY DRUMMOND

Life is a flower of which
love is the honey.

VICTOR HUGO

It is your unlimited power to care
and to love that can make the biggest difference
in the quality of your life.

ANTHONY ROBBINS

We are shaped and fashioned
by what we love.

JOHANN WOLFGANG VON GOETHE

To love and be loved is
to feel the sun
from both sides.

DAVID VISCOTT

Love and a cough
cannot be hid.

GEORGE HERBERT

To love for the sake of being loved is human,
but to love for the sake of loving is angelic.

ALPHONSE DE LAMARTINE

I like not only to be loved,
but also to be told that I am loved.

GEORGE ELIOT

Love begets love.

THEODORE ROETHKE

Love
cannot be wasted.

Love is love's reward.

JOHN DRYDEN

If you would be loved,
love and be loveable.

BENJAMIN FRANKLIN

If there is anything better
than to be loved,
it is to love.

The desire to be beloved is
ever restless and unsatisfied,
but the love that flows out upon others
is a perpetual wellspring from on high.

LYDIA M. CHILD

It may be risky to marry for love,
but it's so honest that the Lord
just has to smile on it.

JOSH BILLINGS

The first duty of love
is to listen.

PAUL TILLICH

Love comforteth like
sunshine after rain.

WILLIAM SHAKESPEARE

No cord or cable can draw so forcibly,
or bind so fast,
as love can do with a single thread.

RICHARD E. BURTON

Down on your knees,
and thank heaven,
fasting, for a good man's love.

WILLIAM SHAKESPEARE

Husbands, love your wives,
even as Christ also loved the church,
and gave himself for it.

EPHESIANS 5:25

Love does not consist of gazing at each other
but in looking together in the same direction.

Antoine De Sainte-Exupery

So ought men to love their wives as their own bodies.
He that loveth his wife loveth himself.

EPHESIANS 5:28

Love is like a pair of socks;
you gotta have two
and they gotta match.

Immature love says,
"I love you because I need you."
Mature love says,
"I need you because I love you."

ERICH FROMM

It is a beautiful necessity
of our nature
to love something.

DOUGLAS JERROLD

I have found the paradox that
if I love until it hurts,
then there is no hurt but only more love.

MOTHER TERESA

Love is
the great miracle cure.

LOUISE HAY

One word frees us of all
the weight and pain of life.
That word is love.

SOPHOCLES

Don't hold to anger,
hurt, or pain;
they steal your energy
and keep you from love.

LEO F. BUSCAGLIA

A good father reflects
the love of
the heavenly Father.

Not father or mother
has loved you as God has,
for it was that you might be happy
He gave His only Son.

HENRY WADSWORTH LONGFELLOW

For whom the Lord loveth he correcteth;
even as a father the son in whom he delighteth.

PROVERBS 3:12

Love is infallible;
it has no errors,
for all the errors are the want of love.

WILLIAM LAW

It is astonishing
how little one feels poverty
when one loves.

EDWARD BULWER-LYTTON

Who, being loved,
is poor?

OSCAR WILDE

Holding the heart of another
in the comforting hands of prayer
is a priceless act of love.

JANET L. WEAVER

The Master,
Who loved most of all,
endured the most and
proved His love by His endurance.

HUGH B. BROWN

They do not love that
do not show their love.

WILLIAM SHAKESPEARE

Love is shown in your deeds,
not in your words.

JEROME CUMMINGS

Love in deed
is love indeed.

Love looks not with the eyes
but with the mind.

WILLIAM SHAKESPEARE

Love is not blind;
it sees more, not less,
but because it sees more,
it chooses to see less.

Blessed is
the influence of one true,
loving soul on another.

GEORGE ELIOT

Joy is the net of love
by which you can catch souls.

MOTHER TERESA

Treasure the love you receive above all.
It will survive long after your gold
and good health have vanished.

OG MANDINO

His creation of you
combined with His love for you
and demonstrated by His work
in you makes you of significant value.

JOSH MCDOWELL

Between whom there is
hearty truth,
there is love.

HENRY DAVID THOREAU

And I have declared
unto them thy name,
and will declare it:
that the love wherewith thou
hast loved me may be in them,
and I in them.

JOHN 17:26

But if any man love God,
the same is known of him.

1 CORINTHIANS 8:3

Many people
mistake our work for our vocation.
Our vocation is the love of Jesus.

MOTHER TERESA

When love and skill work together,
expect a masterpiece.

JOHN RUSKIN

Take away love,
and our earth is a tomb.

ROBERT BROWNING

Love is to the mortal nature
what the sun is to the earth.

HONORE DE BALZAC

Never forget that the
most powerful force
on earth is love.

NELSON ROCKEFELLER

Love doesn't make the world go around;
love is what makes the ride worthwhile.

FRANKLIN P. JONES

For God so loved the world,
that he gave his only begotten Son,
that whosoever believeth in him
should not perish,
but have everlasting life.

JOHN 3:16

Love is
the river of life
in the world.

HENRY WARD BEECHER